REPORTS

OF THE

SOLDIERS' MEMORIAL SOCIETY,

Boston

PRESENTED AT ITS

THIRD ANNUAL MEETING,

JUNE 11, 1867.

PUBLISHED BY ORDER OF THE SOCIETY.

BOSTON:
23 CHAUNCY STREET.
1867.

Soldiers' Memorial Society.

President:

ARTHUR T. LYMAN, Esq.

Vice-Presidents:

Hon. FRANK B. FAY,
Hon. MARTIN BRIMMER,
Col. H. S. RUSSELL,
Gen. CHAS. G. LORING,
Rev. EDW. N. KIRK, D. D.,
Rev. HENRY C. POTTER, D. D.,
Rev. ROLLIN NEALE, D. D.,
E. S. TOBEY, Esq.

Treasurer:

JOHN L. EMMONS, Esq.

Secretary:

H. E. SCUDDER, Esq.

Finance Committee:

JOHN L. EMMONS, Esq.,
Rev. ADAMS AYER,
H. E. SCUDDER, Esq.,
P. UPHAM, Esq.,
Gen. CHAS. G. LORING,
Col. H. S. RUSSELL,
WARREN SAWYER, Esq.,
Rev. T. B. FORBUSH,
J. B. CRAM, Esq.,
Rev. EDW. E. HALE.

Teachers' Committee:

A. T. LYMAN, Esq.,
H. E. SCUDDER, Esq.,
AUGUSTUS LOWELL, Esq.,
Mrs. HELEN GILSON OSGOOD.

Executive Committee:

Gen. CHAS. G. LORING,
A. T. LYMAN, Esq.,
J. L. EMMONS, Esq.,
Rev. H. W. FOOTE,
WM. H. REED, Esq.,
Rev. S. W. BUSH,
Rev. CHARLES LOWE,
Miss M. WIGGLESWORTH,
Mrs. A. HEMENWAY,
Miss HORATIA WARE.

Clothing and Supplies:

Mrs. MANTON EASTBURN,
Mrs. S. T. HOOPER,
Mrs. HELEN GILSON OSGOOD,
Miss A. WIGGLESWORTH,
Mrs. BENJ. PICKMAN,
Mrs. WM. SOHIER,
Miss S. C. WILLIAMS,
Miss I. E. LORING,
Miss E. D. SOUTHWICK.

Memorial Committee:

Rev. EDW. E. HALE,
Hon. F. B. FAY,
Gen. CHAS. G. LORING,
Gen. A. B. UNDERWOOD,
Mrs. WM. SOHIER,
Miss S. CABOT.

SOLDIERS' MEMORIAL SOCIETY.

ANNUAL REPORT OF THE DIRECTORS.

In three successive Reports, which have been printed and circulated at different periods as the year has passed, the Directors have submitted the more important facts regarding the progress of the work in their hands. On the present occasion, it is only necessary to explain, as far as may be, the general system and hope in which we work,—referring to those special reports for detail.

The Soldiers' Memorial Society was founded just at the close of the war, by men and women who had worked in the army and for the army, in the belief that many years would pass by before the wounds of the war would be healed,—that there would be constant and varied necessity for Christian work here in New England for the help of those regions which had been ravaged in war,—and that it would be well to keep close the ties which had united us in the charities of the war, that we might be ready for whatever exigency should still require charities rendered in a kindred spirit. In this view, we abstained, with some care, from limiting the field of our work, either by entangling alliances with other associations, or by the limitations of our own constitution. To lift, wherever we could take hold,—to succor, wherever we had the means, was our purpose; and our judgment here has been confirmed by our experience. The various lines of work which we have undertaken have all been such as we could not have laid out beforehand. They are such as have been suggested by a kind Providence to large hearted men and women who have attempted to carry them through,—and, as we have learned of the plans of these laborers, we have done our best to assist them. Without making promises for the future, we refrain also from binding ourselves merely to the specific work we have done in the past. Our organization is ready for any duty which may offer which the people will give us the means to undertake.

This organization consists of the usual officers of a society, chosen for keeping up its records and correspondence, and for the care of its treasury,—and also of four standing committees. One of these—the Committee of Clothing and Supplies—is in attendance every day, at the office, by one at least of its members, to receive, and report or act upon, each case of destitution or necessity that may be reported. These committees, and the officers from the Board of Directors, which meets on the first Tuesday of every month to receive the reports of the various committees and act on their requisitions, make up our convenient working system.

The Treasurer's Report, annexed to this Report, will show what sum of money has been entrusted to us for the different lines of work we have had in hand. Besides this sum, we have been favored by the steady assistance of the Boston Sewing Circle, which meets every week in the large and convenient room where we are now assembled, and joins us in paying the rent for it. We have received similar assistance and contributions of clothing in very considerable quantities from several other organizations, to whom we return our cordial thanks. Their specific contributions are acknowledged in the Report of the Committee of Clothing and Supplies.

We proceed to enumerate the various points through the South where we have tried to be of use, naming them in geographical order:—

ALEXANDRIA AND PETERSBURG.

At Alexandria, in Virginia, we have employed Mrs. Parker to distribute clothing, and have furnished her with material to be made up by poor women there. This lady, who had acquired a large experience in her work with the army, is engaged in the duties which we know here as the work of "The Ministry at Large." She is referred to by the officers in charge, both of the army and of the city, as a person whose judgment may be relied upon in the care of the poor. A pressing appeal has now come from her for the enlargement of her work,—from her account of which we print an extract in the Appendix to this Report. We must, in passing, express the hope that some friend will enable us to respond favorably to such a call.

It is true, and natural, that the suggestion sometimes arises that such charities as this should be maintained by the people of the place; that they involve local inquiries, are to meet local necessities and must be supplied, therefore, at the local charge. Supposing that this may be true in the natural condition of things, it is however evident, now, that the Southern communities are none of them in the natural condition of things. They are exhausted by the efforts of an unsuccessful war,—in which those resources have been expended which might have been sufficient for the service of many years of peace. To say, then, that a school in Alexandria must be supported by the residents or not at all, is, practically, to say that it shall not be supported at all. Yet the time is exactly the time when such a school is most needed,—as the same causes which bring poverty upon the whole community have so deranged old arrangements for labor as to compel many who are wholly untrained in it to make their own clothing, if they are to have any fit clothing to wear.

We have made a similar distribution of a small invoice of clothing in Petersburg, by the hands of Miss Aikin.

RICHMOND.

We have been solicited to establish free and industrial schools at Fredericksburg, but have not been able to do so; for we determined, at the very beginning of the year, to concentrate our effort, by whatever sacrifice at other points, so as to carry forward as rapidly as possible, and on as liberal a scale as possible, the free-school system of Richmond.

Just at the time when our annual report was presented last year, we received an earnest request, from the head of the Freedmen's Bureau at Richmond, to take in charge the system of schools there known as the Laboratory or Hollywood Schools. We had then attempted, as far as we could, to separate our work from that of literary education, supposing that there were enough societies which had instruction in letters for their only aim to care for such necessities. But a series of complications at Richmond brought about a request from all parties that we would undertake these white schools, and at the annual meeting last year authority was given to the Board of Directors to do so.

The details of their great success have been laid before the Society in successive special reports. The general view on which we have bestowed upon them so much time and money is this. Richmond, for so many years the capital of the Confederacy, is still the city of most influence at the South. The substantial establishment of a well-arranged system of public schools in that city, open freely to all children of all races and conditions, and giving to such children as good instruction as is possible anywhere, would at once attract attention, and would compel imitation. Such a system would very soon be established in all the other large towns of Virginia. From Virginia, also, it would extend itself, almost without effort from the outside, into all the other States which are still proud to take pattern from Virginia.

But such an establishment, either to be studied or to be copied, must be large enough to attract attention and extend widely enough to answer the general purposes of a free-school system. It must provide, in especial, for all the working classes, black and white; for the working men must be taught by it that the triumph of free institutions is their triumph,—and that they received the greatest blessing possible on the day of the final triumph of the National arms.

In large measure, we believe these results have been secured at Richmond, under the arrangements for the completion of which our schools are necessary. While the Freedmen's Commission and other societies maintain enough free schools for the education of about four thousand black children, our schools are sufficient for the education of near seven hundred white children. The aggregate, it is true, is not more than one third, if it is so much, of the number of children in the town. But the habit of school attendance by all is yet to be formed,—and, in the steady increase of the number of schools, there is always kept open the hope to those not now provided for that full provision is not far off. In proportion, also, as they "wish there were more," is their attention turned to the only permanent method of sustaining such schools, namely, by the vote of the people who are to use them.

The prime object, never lost sight of by the Directors or by the teachers, has been to interest the people of Richmond, practically, in a free-school system. With this view, we have spared no expense to bring our schools to the highest standard known to us. We believe that we have been particularly successful in our selection of a corps of teachers. Mr. Washburn, who is at the head of the establishment, Mrs. Washburn, and the staff of ladies employed, have worked at their great duty with an enthusiasm which showed that they understood its importance, and with such discretion and steadiness as have commanded success. The consequence has been that our schools have received the highest commendation from the citizens of Richmond and from strangers visiting that city. Every school has been pressed by applicants wishing to attend, far beyond its capacity. On occasion of the absence of a child for a few days from its seat, there has always been some one in waiting to take the coveted privilege as long as it could be even temporarily secured. We have reason to believe that the schools for colored children, which are not under our charge, have been kept up to a very high standard. The result of this general free education, of a type quite different from anything which any other schools in Richmond could exhibit, has been a new and general interest in free public instruction among the people of that city. Free public instruction is now demanded in the manifestoes of every political party; and we are assured that no measures for the re-adjustment of the political status of Virginia can succeed which do not recognize, as a fundamental necessity, free public instruction.

We hoped, at the beginning of the course, to provide in advance for this public movement in Virginia, by the establishment of a normal school, for the proper education of teachers. Our friends of the Freedmen's Commission have had a similar wish. But the pressure on both societies, for elementary instruction, has been too great to enable us fully to carry out our plans. It is with great satisfaction, therefore, that we learn that a number of the most intelligent and far-sighted citizens of Richmond have undertaken the establishment of such a school, by an organization among themselves, in anticipation of the time, which must not be far off, when the city council shall take the full charge of such an establishment. The Directors recommend to their successors the most diligent encouragement of this promising movement.

In all such enterprises as ours, it is to be remembered, that the National Government, acting through the Bureau of Freedmen and Refugees, is the great benefactor of the Southern States. Our efforts, and those of all the aid societies, are almost insignificant, in comparison with the determined and steady care, oversight and assistance rendered by the Nation. It is to be understood, therefore, in all that we say of our Richmond schools, that, from the beginning, the Government has furnished the necessary buildings, has assisted us in furnishing them, has given transportation to our teachers, and in every way where we have asked the coöperation of the Bureau, has rendered its assistance and support to the enterprise we have had in hand. We have been especially indebted, in Richmond, to the friendly offices of General Brown, who is fortunately at the head of the Bureau there.

At the request of General Brown, made to us in the autumn, we assumed the charge of the Orphan Asylum instituted for the relief of colored orphans. This establishment had been under the direction of the Society of Friends, who had, at that time however, relinquished it. Our friends at Worcester, in this State, undertook the pecuniary charges of this very interesting charity. We need not undertake here to enter into the details, as to the difficulties of rightly managing it. It is in the hands of a special Committee of our Board, and we trust that those difficulties are diminishing under their careful administration, and that the temporary need for the establishment is lessened daily, as the pacification of the country goes forward.

HAMPTON, VA.

In answer to an application from the head of the Bureau at Hampton, for the establishment of a school there, of which a part of the expense should be borne by the citizens, we sent Miss Emma D. and Miss Abby Southwick thither, to establish an industrial school and a common school. They have been engaged in this work for a few months only, but with marked success.

WILMINGTON, N. C.

In attempting to carry forward the whole system of white schools at Richmond, we at first thought it prudent to give up, however unwillingly, the promising beginning which we had made by Mr. Thurston at Wilmington, that, as we have said, we might concentrate our effort at the old capital of the Confederacy. But on urgent representations from the people of Wilmington, both of the necessity of the school which we had opened and the certainty that, without help from us, it would not be resumed, we commissioned Miss Amy Bradley to go to Wilmington and to take charge of a part of the pupils in the schoolhouse, of which we had secured the use. Miss Bradley was also to devote such time and attention as she could to an industrial school. She has pressed her work with such energy as to secure the coöperation of the people in the enlargement of the schoolhouse,—and we have been glad to be able to meet her call for two assistant teachers. Their letters give the most gratifying accounts of their success.

HARKER'S ISLAND, N. C.

The work of Miss Bell, at Harker's Island, enlists our hearty interest; and we must hope that larger assistance may be given her next year than we have had in our power to give this. On an island inhabited by the poorest class of "poor whites," she has established herself, resolved, by teaching them to work, by teaching their children to read, and by introducing habits of industry, order and temperance, that she will lift them out of the semi-barbarous condition of sloth and beggary in which she found them. Her energy and courage alone deserve all the aid we can give to her; and the remarkable success she has already attained shows that her good judgment is equal to her energy and courage. We have used such influence as we could in inducing others to assist her, and have been able to send to her some boxes of clothing. We believe there is no more interesting work now in progress in the Southern country.

CHARLESTON, S. C.

At Charleston, we have continued the work of the Industrial Rooms under charge of Mrs. Ringgold, who has been, as we believe, singularly successful in her charitable labors among the destitute, and in her determination to put them in the way of caring for themselves. Some friends have contributed something for her Poor's Purse, also.

We forwarded to General Sickles, for the general relief, some boxes of clothing; and were able to meet some other calls recommended to us by individuals.

OTHER POINTS.

The report of the Committee on Clothing and Supplies shows, in detail, what assistance we have been able to render in answer to calls from Hendersonville, N. C.; Pendleton, S. C.; Savannah, Ga.; Port Orange and Gordon, in Florida. These are illustrations of the classes of relief and of suffering to which it is our wish that we may always be able to respond. We believe that such an organization as we have formed can attend to them more promptly, more intelligently and more economically than would be possible if each case of distress had to present its own appeal, and secure its own answer from the community. We are gratified that we have been able to meet so many calls, and we hope that in another year it may be in our power to meet more.

THE LOYAL PRESS.

We had presented to us last year, appeals, in different forms, from Fredericksburg, from Richmond, from Wilmington, from Savannah, from Augusta, from Florida and from Memphis, asking in each case that we would lend our influence and assistance for the establishment of loyal newspapers in those cities. All these appeals were referred to a sub-committee, and this sub-committee conferred with gentlemen who had taken an active part in the management of the Loyal Publication Society. This Committee reported to the Directors that this Society could not assume any direct part in carrying forward these enterprises. But we have been able, in three of the cases referred to, to give proper direction and recommendation to the parties most interested. In all these cases the desired object has been attained. It must be steadily remembered, while we are teaching the people of the South to read, that the duty of next importance is supplying, at once, the cheap and popular reading which they may use to their profit as soon as they have learned their lesson.

COLLEGES AND HIGH SCHOOLS.

We have received several applications, all of an interesting character, to assist colleges and high schools which propose the higher education of the people of the Southwest. All of these institutions make their claim to us on the ground that they will educate teachers who will be of use in educating others. This is the only claim they can make, for we have no interest in continuing longer the old mistaken system of the South, which considered education a boon for the higher classes only, to which the poor were not entitled. It is gratifying to observe, that in every appeal thus made to us we have full assurance that the education of the black as well as the white race is to be attended to, and precisely the same facilities given to one as to the other. In no case have we made an appropriation for any of these schools. But we have examined the testimonials carefully which have been presented, and have introduced the principals of the schools to such persons as could best assist them. Such inquiry, on our part, as to the real designs and means of those who seek help in New England, serves one important object of our organization.

HOWARD INDUSTRIAL SCHOOL AT CAMBRIDGE.

At the suggestion of Miss Anne Lowell, at that time an active member of our Board, a Committee was appointed, of which she was the head, to enter into correspondence with officers of the Freedmen's Bureau, in those centres where negro laborers most congregated, with reference to systematic arrangements for the humane transportation of women and children from such places to this part of the country. This Committee took charge of these arrangements, in concert with the Bureau officers, until it appeared advisable to erect the system thus founded, into an independent organization, under the name of the Howard Industrial School for Colored Women and Girls, now successfully established at Cambridge.

We look on this undertaking as a most valuable instrumentality in the adjustment of the disturbed condition of affairs. While there is great want of labor here, particularly of domestic servants, there is an overplus of such labor at the South. It is as certain, as that water runs down hill, that the overplus will come into the vacant place, where it is needed. Any effort to keep it out is like Mrs. Partington's to sweep back the sea. The only questions are, whether these poor women and children shall suffer every extortion, as all ignorant emigrants do of necessity, and whether employers here must meet great inconvenience in obtaining labor, which needs employment; or whether, by as simple arrangement as that made by the Howard School, women and children shall come here without being starved and cheated, and employers be able to contract with them, without making in each case difficult and complicated arrangements for their transportation.

In closing this Report, the Directors have to renew the expression of their hearty thanks to all the teachers and other persons employed, to all the sewing societies which have coöperated with us, to the contributors to our treasury, to the directors of the journals of Boston, Worcester, Providence and Lowell, to the officers of the Boston Gas Light Company, who for some months gave us our office rent free, to the American Tract Society, the Sunday School Union, and the Sunday School Society, to the officers of the Freedmen's Bureau, and to all other persons who have assisted in the work of our Society. From those of small means we have received gifts as cheerfully offered as the contributions made in larger sums.

Respectfully submitted, by

EDW. E. HALE, *Secretary.*

June 11, 1867.

TREASURER'S REPORT.

SOLDIERS' MEMORIAL SOCIETY *in account with* JOHN L. EMMONS, *Treasurer.*

DR.

June, 1866.	To Cash, Paid	for support of Schools at Richmond, Va. - -	$5,734 84	
	" "	Schools at Wilmington, N. C.,	377 60	
	" "	Industrial Home, Charleston, S. C. - - -	526 00	
	" "	at other localities at the South	86 96	
	" "	Clothing and Supply Committee, chiefly for forwarding	155 00	
	" "	Office expenses, salary of agent, rent, printing, travelling, &c.	1,076 26	
	Balance to credit, on new account, - -		756 86	
				$8,713 52

Cr.

June, 1866.	By Cash,	of A. T. Lyman, late Treas., balance of account - - - -	$11 02
	"	Misses Wigglesworth - - -	500 00
	"	Charles G. Loring - - -	125 00
	"	New Bedford Freedmen and White Refugees' Society - - -	500 00
	"	Walpole, Ms., First Parish Ladies' Society, (in part) - - -	250 00
	"	Waltham, Ms. - - - -	240 00
	"	West Church, Dr. Bartol - -	280 75
	"	Rev. Dr. Putnam's Society, Roxbury	237 00
	"	Mrs. Pollard - - - -	2 50
	"	H. S's subscription, per N. P. Russell	100 00
	"	Mrs. H. F. Wolcott - - -	50 00
	"	Samuel D. Warren - - -	500 00
	"	A. T. Lyman - - - -	100 00
	"	Friend, Springfield, Ms. - -	10 00
	"	Miss H. Ware - - - -	5 00
	"	Mrs. S. L. Sohier - - -	50 00
	"	Misses Lowell, Roxbury - -	50 00
	"	Rev. C. C. Sulter, West Cambridge -	5 00
	"	H. P. Nichols - - - -	75 00
	"	J. J. Low - - - -	20 00
	"	Greely S. Curtis - - -	200 00
	"	George A. Goddard - - -	50 00
	"	Rev. George Putnam - - -	50 00
	"	Miss S. C. Williams - - -	20 00
	"	Adams Ayer - - - -	100 00
	"	John J. Dixwell - - -	100 00
	"	Henry Callender - - -	50 00
	"	Miss Newman - - - -	100 00
	"	Francis Amory - - -	50 00
	"	Five members Unitarian Society, West Cambridge - - - -	47 00
	"	E. W. Hooper, Treas. N. E. Branch Freedmen's and Union Comm. in full for School building, Richmond	250 00
	"	Wm. Endicott, Jr. - - -	100 00
	"	A friend - - - -	15 00
	"	" Dover, N. H. - -	5 00
	"	Henry B. Rogers - - -	100 00
	"	Town of Beverly - - -	164 00
	"	Thomas Gaffield - - -	25 00
	"	Unitarian Society, West Roxbury, T. B. Forbush, pastor - - -	105 20

Cr.

1866. By Cash,	Rev. C. A. Humphrey, Springfield, Mass.	$72 00
"	Mrs. E. J. Newell - - - -	5 00
"	Mrs. J. L. Gray - - - -	10 00
"	Charles G. Loring, Jr. - - -	100 00
"	John L. Emmons - - - -	50 00
1867. By Cash,	S. Austin Harris - - - -	5 00
"	Mrs. Augustus Hemenway - -	250 00
"	Charles Follen - - - -	50 00
"	Henry P. Kidder - - - -	100 00
"	Miss M. G. Chapman - - -	3 00
"	A Friend - - - - -	50 00
"	Miss Martha Brooks - - -	5 00
"	Field, Convers & Allen - - -	100 00
"	Dr. E. H. Clarke - - - -	10 00
"	Francis H Peabody - - -	50 00
"	Friend - - - - -	1 05
"	J. B. Cram - - - - -	25 00
"	H. S. Russell - - - -	50 00
"	Mrs. Charles G. Loring - - -	50 00
"	Mrs. W. S. Whitwell - - -	20 00
"	J. Wiley Edmands - - - -	100 00
"	A Friend of Southern education - -	10 00
"	H. B. Taylor - - - -	25 00
"	A. G. Farwell & Co. - - -	25 00
"	Edward Wyman - - - -	25 00
"	Two Ladies, per H. P. Kidder - -	250 00
"	Theo. Lyman - - - -	25 00
"	Waldo Higginson - - - -	10 00
"	Miss M. A. Wales - - - -	100 00
"	Citizens of Littleton, Ms. - - -	29 00
"	William Gray - - - -	100 00
"	C. Wm. Loring - - - -	50 00
"	John A. Loring - - - -	20 00
"	Augustus Lowell - - - -	200 00
"	John A. Lowell - - - -	200 00
"	Hollis Street Society, (in part) - -	300 00
"	David L. Webster - - - -	50 00
"	John G. Webster - - - -	25 00
"	A friend for Southern enlightenment -	70 00
"	Ladies' Charitable Society, Groton, Ms. -	5 00
"	King's Chapel Society - 795 00	
	Less, credited to individuals elsewhere, &c. - - 130 00—	665 00
"	Misses J. & E. May - - - -	100 00

CR.

1867.	By Cash,	Count Schwabe	$10 00	
	"	Church of the Unity, Worcester, (in part)	200 00	
	"	A Friend of Southern education	20 00	
	"	Mrs. J. A. Lowell	50 00	
	"	Mrs. Manton Eastburn	10 00	
	"	Martin Brimmer	100 00	
	"	Friends, for Charleston, S. C.	26 00	
	"	Sale of three rebel desks	15 00	
	"	H. E. Scudder	150 00	
	"	John M. Forbes	100 00	
				$8,713 52
June 1, 1867.	By balance as per contra			$756 86

BOSTON, 1 JUNE, 1867.

E. E.,
JOHN L. EMMONS.

NOTE. In this account are not included the share of rent paid by joint-occupants of our rooms, nor a few small amounts paid to one of the Committees, for specific purposes, and expended by them.

REPORT OF THE COMMITTEE ON CLOTHING AND SUPPLY, FOR THE YEAR ENDING JUNE 11, 1867.

The Committee on Clothing and Supply report that they have received

NEW GARMENTS.

From the	Boston Sewing Circle	3,683
"	South Friendly Society, (Rev. E. E. Hale's)	224
"	Mayhew Society, (Dr. Bartol) for Mrs. Jacob's Hospital	42
"	Hollis Street Charitable Union	20
"	Ladies of the Channing Circle, Newton Corner	70
"	First Parish in Walpole, (with box of books)	6
"	First Parish in Groton	21
"	Ladies of the Asylum, Somerville, prs. socks	36
"	Watertown and Belmont, through Mrs. Titcomb	54
"	Three Ladies in Jamaica Plain, for Florida	81
"	"for the poor of the South," through Mrs. Curtis	23
"	Others	26
On hand June 5, 1866, as per report		1,211
	Total	5,497

These have been forwarded for distribution, as follows:—

To Richmond, Va., to the Industrial School, under charge of Andrew Wasburn, Superintendent of Schools - -	1,303
Alexandria, Va., Mrs. M. N. Parker - - - -	425
Petersburg, Va., Miss A. Aiken - - - -	149
Hampton, Va., Miss E. D. Southwick - - -	303
Wilmington, N. C., Industrial School, under charge of Miss Amy M. Bradley - - - - - -	522
Harker's Island, N. C., Miss J. S. Bell - - -	201
Hendersonville, N. C., Mrs. J. H. Allen, for Unionists -	79
Charleston, S. C., House of Industry, Mrs. M. C. Ringgold -	605
" " for general relief, through General Sickles	331
" " for special relief, through Mrs. Boutelle -	22
Pendleton, S. C., Rev. T. H. Edwards, Orphan Asylum -	243
Savannah, Ga., Mrs. Jacobs, for hospital - - -	169
Port Orange, Volusia Co., Fa., Mrs. E. H. Hawkes - -	191
Gordon, Fa., Mr. R. James - - - - - -	201
the sufferers by the fire, at Portland, Me. - - -	*586
On hand, packed - - - - - - - -	167
Total - - - - - - - -	5,497

In addition to the above, twelve boxes of clothing have been received and forwarded, unopened, to the various Schools under the Superintendence of Mr. Washburn, at Richmond. From the Freedmen and White Refugees' Aid Society at New Bedford, to Miss Howard, nine; from the Society at Walpole, to Miss Morse, three.

Also, not included in the above list, were numerous bundles or boxes of second-hand clothing, from Sherborn, and other places, many of them sent anonymously.

They very gratefully acknowledge the receipt of:—

54 yards blue flannel from Messrs. Dale Bros. & Co.; 126 1-2 yards sheeting, from Messrs. Jordan, Marsh & Co.; 207 1-4 yards sheeting and 315 3-4 yards calico, from Messrs. J. C. Howe & Co.; and a large number of packing cases from Messrs. Spalding, Hay & Wales.

From Mrs. Loring, for Florida, 42 yards cotton, 41 calico, groceries, books and seeds. From the Boston Sewing Circle, for Charleston, 7 pieces of cotton, 6 of calico, and from a friend for the same destination, one piece of cotton. From Mrs. Lowell, a carpet, and many donations of minor importance from various sources.

Of another class of gifts that have been of material aid in our educational efforts at the South, have been:—

* These garments were made by the ladies of the Boston Sewing Circle, and were sent to Portland as soon as the fire of July 4, 1866, took place, at their direction.

Three boxes of books for Sunday schools, from Dr. Putnam's Society through Rev. A. Ayer; one box from the North Church Sunday school, Salem; one box each from Misses Lowell, Miss Fette, Rev. Mr. Snow, Marshfield, Mr. M. F. Hunnewell, Roxbury, from the First Parish in Walpole, from the Ladies' Commission, from the South Congregational Church, from Hollis Street Sunday school; three from the Christian Register Office; and numerous smaller packages.

Also, from Mr. J. Bumstead, 405 primers and other school-books; from Mr. J. L. Shorey, 75 school-books and a set of charts; from Messrs. Brewer & Tileston, 24 school-books; from Mr. T. O. H. P. Burnham, 64 school-books, and about 250 Sunday school-books; from Messrs. Hoyt and Kemp, 2 packages Sunday school-books and cards; from the Bible Society, 62 Testaments and 12 copies Gospel of St. John; from the American Tract Society, and the Sunday School Society, books and papers. These have been used in the various schools established by the Society.

A promiscuous assortment of second hand school-books, received from various sources, has been distributed to needy schools in Virginia and Georgia. From Count Schwabè we have been favored with some fifty volumes of books for prizes in the schools.

The Ladies of the Universalist Church at Arlington have very kindly aided in making up garments and preparing work for the Sewing schools.

In returning thanks to all who have aided them, and especially to the Ladies of the Boston Sewing Circle, the almoners of whose liberal-handed charity they have been, the Committee assure the donors that their benefactions have succored and blessed a needy and suffering people, who by these means often have been brought to hold as friends those whom they had accounted enemies. In doing a work of charity they have helped, in a way not to be misunderstood or undervalued, to a solution of the great problem of reconstruction.

To their own, the Committee can add the thanks of the teachers and agents at the South, who have thus been enabled to alleviate a destitution very painful to witness, and who have found the power of relieving physical distress a very important auxiliary in their efforts for the education and moral improvement of the people of the South.

The Committee also report that they have received from several ladies, most of whose names appear in the Treasurer's report as contributors of larger amounts, the sum of $160,—for objects especially named, chiefly for the "poor fund" of Mrs. Ringgold, at Charleston, which has been expended as directed.

For the Committee,

CHAS. G. LORING, Jr., *Chairman.*

APPENDIX.

The passages from Reports and letters, which we copy below, will indicate the character of our work in its detail:

I. Schools at Richmond.

From letter of Andrew Washburn, Superintendent.

Richmond, Va., Dec. 1, 1866.

The down town school is appreciated by the poor already, and the opening of the other grades anxiously waited for. Such instances as this are of frequent occurrence: a laboring man brought in his two boys of about 10 and 12 years, and introduced them as "two poor boys who had not known a day's schooling since the war." He could not afford to send them to the pay schools, and there were no others to which they could go. This city is full of such.

From the same.

Richmond, Va., Jan. 1, 1867.

I think I see considerable increase of interest in educational matters in the city. Our schools are known and quoted often, but, after the true southern spirit, they try to show interest in education in their own way. They try to brush up the old "Lancastrian" school, and solicit pupils from us and are making strenuous efforts to have this school better, or supposed better than ours. We have lost one scholar thus far. The Masonic fraternity has just opened a "Free Academy," quite near us, likewise. The yeast is working, but the effort is to make the old system supply the new demand. It is the old story of new wine in old bottles. The question here is, how can the wine be saved?

With the cold weather the calls for charity are multiplied; no day passes without a large number from both white and black. The contributions of the "branches," in addition to supplies received from you, enable us to respond in part to some of the most urgent. I have also succeeded, in several cases, in obtaining aid from the government, for whites as well as blacks. Still there is, and is likely to be, much suffering, even among the comparatively few Union people here; I mean, among those who were Union during the war.

From the same.

RICHMOND, VA., Jan. 10, 1867.

I am glad the "Despatch" pleased you. The papers are well disposed to us. I think, in fact we have quite a constituency here, and are getting to be a political power. In the schools and in the shops I say to all who tell me "the State ought to give us 'Free Schools,'" "just require of the man you send to the Assembly to pledge himself to favor a Free School system."

From the same.

RICHMOND, VA., Jan. 30, 1867.

We are now sending away many from the Lowell School, not being able to accommodate all who come. On Monday some fourteen, and others yesterday, could not be received. There are a large number applying for Church-hill, and I am very sorry that you think another teacher doubtful.

Miss Breck has retained seventy-two in her school, and will feel the loss of Miss Parker (who was to be assigned to the new school at Church-hill) seriously. I do hope for another teacher.

From the same.

RICHMOND, VA., Feb. 1, 1867.

Church-hill comes on finely, but takes all my time and will for a few days. School will commence there on Monday next. I think we shall be quite full there very soon. There will be a large Union element in the school. I shall take first the children of the "Union Refugees" and then fill up in order of application.

From the same.

RICHMOND, VA., March 7, 1867.

We endeavor to turn the public attention to the importance of general education, and our schools are an acknowledged centre of influence in favor of a Public School system.

Our work is well received. The schools are full, with long lists of applicants waiting for admission; and many and earnest petitions are received asking for schools at other points in the city, and through the State.

The Richmond "press" has never given us an unfavorable criticism.

From the same.

RICHMOND, VA., March 27, 1867.

I am glad to receive the supplies, both because they relieve actual suffering, and because also it gives influence and power to our endeavors educationally.

I have never been so besieged as at present, by those asking aid to get work, or rations, or clothing, or transportation to where work may be obtained.

From the same.

RICHMOND, VA., June 3, 1867.

It is of the utmost importance that we keep up our work until the new order of things in Virginia is fixed. Now is the formative time. The next year will settle the principles, and the next following the practice of the new regime, and then our work is done, and the status of Virginia is fixed for a generation at least.

We look to the presence of our schools, more than to any single means, to turn hatred into love, and to put in place of the old disregard of the education of the masses, and their consequent deplorable ignorance, a system by which the State shall assume the responsibility to educate her every child.

Letter from Mrs. E. G. Washburn.

RICHMOND, VA., Jan. 8, 1867.

To-day I have had my first Sewing School. The children and their parents have manifested much interest in this, and although in the midst of a regular N. E. snowstorm, a very fair attendance cheered my first attempt. We have Miss Haskell's school-room, and a very light pleasant room it is. We can see to work until nearly five o'clock. We shall meet each afternoon except Wednesday and Saturday. I invite them to bring their own work, *just as far as possible.* After finding out the resources of a particular family, I proposed to one to make a bed quilt, another to learn to *mend* or *darn.* Some few have handkerchiefs to hem, or new garments to make. I want all to feel it a school for instruction rather than charity. Some come without any work, and for these I provided, by help of a donation received from Waltham, of twenty yards of cloth, thread and needles.

Mr. Washburn says, the enterprise must *not be expensive*, and I can't see why it need be. There may be cases where I shall wish to set a little girl to making patchwork, or even garments, who can't find the material, and who had better have the squares when finished, or the garment because she needs it, rather than because she made it, but I shall endeavor to fit the children just as far as may be, for every day work, by encouraging them to bring of the family work as it comes along from day to day.

Here let me acknowledge the receipt of the much longed for box sent by you. I had many waiting and shivering for the arrival of the clothing. The books are *splendid*, real *readable* books; we were delighted with them, and the Sabbath school rejoiced over them in a way that was very pleasant to see.

From the same.

RICHMOND, VA., Feb. 15, 1867.

The Sewing School is a *success* in every sense of the word; I don't know what I could wish to have different about it, unless it is more instructors. It numbers ninety different pupils, and *every* day we have between fifty and sixty present.

I find that all bring work who have anything to bring, but there are a good many who have nothing unless I give it to them. All this time we have used thread, etc., that came from Waltham, but these were nearly exhausted when relief came from you. The same day I also received a quantity of cloth and a dress pattern from Waltham. People do respond wonderfully to calls made by us, and I feel now that I can see the way clear in the Sewing school for the present. The parents are much interested in the school—some have even gone so far as to ask if *they* could not come; but the children require every moment of the time, and must have it. We must teach them thrift, taste, economy, ingenuity, and, most of all, neatness.

I like to make the school as cheerful as possible, and so, (for instance,) last Friday afternoon, as I had but little help I thought to vary the employment of the last half hour, I would have them sing and invite Miss Breck's drawing class of boys to hear them. The girls have been trained by Miss Foster and sing sweetly. We sent our compliments to Miss B. and her class, and after a little amusing delay, occasioned by the young lads making as fine a toilet as they could with washing their hands and faces, and brushing their hair, Miss B. marshalled them in. They were exceedingly flustered at first, but soon recovered. I asked them during the exercise if they would prefer any particular piece—my immediate answer was, "The red, white and blue." It was well and spiritedly rendered, and every thing passed off very pleasantly.

This may seem of little account to you, but I can see good effects from meeting in this way upon the manners of the children.

From Miss Sarah E. Foster.

RICHMOND, VA., NOV. 3, 1866.

I had hardly been in the city twenty-four hours ere a little girl, and one of my former pupils, and who followed me to the station when I left Richmond, found my whereabouts.

It was really touching to witness her manifestations of delight at meeting me again. The tears rolling down her cheeks, and sobbing out her words of welcome. I felt, if she were the only one to welcome me, I was well repaid for all the sacrifice in coming again.

She spread the news that *Teacher* had come, and I could hardly find time to unpack my trunk, for receiving the calls of the dear children.

I could hardly believe they had waited and watched so anxiously for my return, as it appeared from their conversation.

One girl who was out at service, for '*Maw*' needed her wages, she said, came with the child who is under her care, and assured me she would come to school if possible, when the month was up.

One of the elder girls, and a perfect treasure in school, came with a beautiful bunch of roses, and offered them with so much affection beaming in her eyes that I could hardly tell which was the more beautiful, the flowers or the giver.

The parents have called upon me, and assured me of their gratitude for what is being done for their children, and I find that Hollywood Free Schools, are becoming an institution.

From the same.

RICHMOND, VA., Dec. 12, 1866.

By visiting these people in their troubles and sorrows we gain their affection and gratitude, and the pleasure they manifest, and the great respect with which we are treated, show that they do appreciate what we are doing. I am sure they are grateful, both for the schools, and for what we can do in supplying their temporal wants.

I called upon a lady who sends two bright eyed girls to my school. She applied to us for clothing and food last winter, and we did all we could for her. She is a sister of the Hon. * * * * formerly member of Congress from Va., and has evidently seen better days. In thanking me for the interest I had taken in her children, she said, "If I had all the money I want, I would send my children to free schools; you take so much more pains with them than they do at pay schools."

These expressions we hear from all quarters, and they are certainly encouraging to us, and I feel that our schools are gaining a firmer foothold on Virginia soil every day.

[Speaking of Mr. S. D. Warren, who pays her salary, she says:]—He visited Richmond last winter, and both teacher and scholars have reason to remember the visit with deep gratitude. The teacher for the encouraging words he gave her, and the children for the very liberal manner in which he remembered their wants.

We rally under the name of the Warren School, and I feel that the children will yet do honor to the name that breathes of New England's patriotism and devotion.

From Miss Sarah E. Haskell.

RICHMOND, VA., Feb. 1, 1867.

We receive a hearty welcome in the *homes* of these children. It is in this way that we may read them aright. The parents express many thanks for the *privilege*, as they term it, of placing their children under our care.

One old lady, upon whom I recently called, inquired how the teachers of the free schools were supported — if it was not done by the city? Upon being told that their maintenance was due to the benevolence of friends at the *North*, her gratitude knew no bounds. She said that it was *mighty good* of the North to take so much interest in the poor Southerners. The *North* had *always* been better to her than the *South*, as she expressed it.

From Miss Rebecca Breck.

RICHMOND, VA., Nov. 16, 1866.

On the day of our removal from Hollywood, I went to the old school-room to meet the boys, that we might take leave of it cheerfully, with songs. There was an old woodcut of Gen. Grant upon the wall. The boys proposed to take it down and transfer it to our new school-room; I liked little to interfere with their partiality for Gen. Grant, but still less that the walls of my school-room should be disfigured by so bad a likeness of him; so I told them, that we would leave it where it hung, and have a good one for our new school-room. Let some of our friends at the North make my promise good, I beg. One day, as I passed the desk of a pupil, I noticed that he put his hand over a picture upon his slate; "Let me look at it," I said. He removed his hand and displayed, with some pride, a rude drawing of the United States flag. "How many stars have you there?" I asked. "The confederate flag has seven," said he. "Is that your flag?" I asked. "No," he answered proudly, "mine has thirty-six."

From the same.

RICHMOND, VA., March 3, 1867.

The Roman Catholic priests have forbidden the children of their Church to attend Protestant schools. If the children obey them, as many of them will, of course, we shall lose many pupils. Some of the parents are very indifferent to the threats of the priests, and others, who are really sincere in their religious faith, hesitate about removing their children from school. One little girl, in Miss Haskell's room, entreated so persistently for permission to remain with Miss Haskell, rather than go to the "Sisters" for instruction, that her father was led to consider the comparative amount and value of information gained at the two schools. He questioned her concerning her studies, and at the end of the examination declared that she had learned more in a month with Miss H. than she would have learned in a year at the Sisters' School. Still, he did not dare disobey the priests; yet poor Katy, though in great trouble at the thought of leaving her beloved teacher, still cherishes a faint hope that her father may "break his mind," as she expresses it.

From Miss Jennie E. Howard.

RICHMOND, VA., Jan. 30, 1867.

There is a great need of more teachers here,—the people seem waking up to the advantage and necessity of free schools here; and many seek admission, but are obliged to be turned away, for want of room.

In my division, I have a class of more than thirty, who read in the Second Reader, study Mental Arithmetic and Geography. I was a little astonished that I should become so much attached to these children, but there is such a warmth of feeling, such an eager, earnest desire to comply with requirements, that one cannot help feeling intensely interested in them. I think I may be the more particularly struck with this manifestation on their part, as I had been led to indulge in expectations far to the contrary.

In visiting among the families of our pupils, we meet with many pleasing incidents, frequently with a stanch Union family, which I assure you is very cheering,— for friendly words are doubly prized here, even though they may come from the poorest, and *apparently* the most forsaken of earth's children.

From Miss M. A. Parker.

RICHMOND, VA., Jan. 28, 1867.

Poverty seems to be a great obstacle in the way of improvement, in the school-room, and it *certainly* is in the *homes* of our pupils. They come to us thinly clad, with pale, pinched faces — suffering, I know, from hunger and cold.

From the same.

RICHMOND, VA., June 3, 1867.

There has been a great deal of sickness among our pupils, during the past winter, in consequence of exposure to the weather. They persist in coming to school through long dreary storms, when poorly clad, and with insufficient covering for the feet. Their interest during the warm weather does not diminish. Many children, who a year ago knew little or nothing of books, have learned to read intelligently, write legibly, if not handsomely; and have mastered the fundamental rules of arithmetic. The influence for good of the schools, upon the morals of the pupils, is very great.

Now a lie is considered a mean thing, and a boy who brings tobacco to school is frowned upon by all his comrades. The code of honor, of the Grammar School, has been brought up to a high standard, by Miss Breck's never failing patience and faithfulness. One boy who *would* cling to old habits, and tried to distract the attention of his neighbors from their studies, was ignored by every boy of his class, till he concluded that no one but himself was injured by his foolishness. He then changed his course and behaved properly.

From Miss E. G. Stanwood.

RICHMOND, VA., June 1, 1867.

I beg leave to submit to you the following report of the Church-hill Schools, for the month just ended. The whole number of pupils has been one hundred and eight. Seven have left school, and we enter on the present month with one hundred and one.

I wrote in my last that I had a list of about sixty applicants whom I could not admit. There have not been many additions to it during the last month, it being well understood that I have no more room. One boy, Mosell Stutz, whose name was put down long ago, has for the last three weeks presented himself almost every day for admission. A few days since, his mother sent word she would pay his tuition if I would take him. Again I had to refuse, but the next day one of the boys left, and although Mosell's name was not next in order, Mr. Washburn advised taking him, as he had been so persistent.

His elder brother waited nearly as long and patiently. One boy who has waited a long time brought me a lovely bouquet of flowers one morning, and preferred his petition: "Please let me come to school?" It was hard to say no, but there was no room for him. When I told one woman I had no seat for her boy, she answered, "Oh he shall bring a seat." Then I had to tell her there was no room for the seat, and she went sadly home. If it is possible, there must be another school in that district next year. The scholars are all ready. Who will send us a teacher, and pay for a room?

II. SCHOOLS AT WILMINGTON.

From Miss A. M. Bradley.

WILMINGTON, N. C., Jan. 15, 1867.

I have a school in the morning of fifty pupils, could have one hundred. Next week I open the Industrial School, with the prospect of double that number. I shall start my Sunday School next Sabbath.

If our people wish to win Wilmington over to the right, now is their opportunity. Only one thing I fear, and that is—that my health will not admit of my teaching. And in the eyes of the people the school for learning to read, etc., is beyond, above everything else. They cannot bear the thought that the colored children are learning more than the white children.

From the same.

WILMINGTON, N. C., March 2, 1867.

It is with pleasure that I take my pen to report the state of the "Industrial School," known as "The Young Ladies' Union Benevolent Society;" which numbers thirty-three members. It was organized January 30th. "The object of the Society is mutual improvement and benefit, and to render aid to the poor wherever we may find them."

President, MISS ALICE L. BENSON.

Secretary and Treasurer, MISS AMY L. BRADLEY.

[Then follows a list of Assistant Cutters, Visiting Committee, &c.]

This Committee is divided so that two of the number, only, accompany me on my visits to the poor "at a time," say, two to-day—next Saturday other two. Saturday is our day for visiting, as we have no school that day. Our days for meeting:—Monday, Wednesday and Friday afternoons, from half past two o'clock until five. Our first box which the Society sent, arrived on the 16th of February. So you will see that the materials for work have been wanting until then.

January 1, 1867, I was a stranger amongst strange people, with clouds in the sky and frost in the natural atmosphere; also, a cloudy sky and a chilling atmosphere in the mental surroundings. March 1, 1867, mark the difference! The days are balmy and sunshiny as a May day, or day in June at the North; I have a day school of seventy-five pupils thoroughly organized and classified; an industrial school of thirty-three, and a Sunday school. Verily our Heavenly Father has given His angels charge over me! Blessed be His name!

From the same.

WILMINGTON, N. C., March 16, 1867.

Miss Gerrish is with me, and relieves me much in my day school—which numbers seventy-five pupils. We have received a present from thirty-four gentlemen of this city, of $99.50, which has enabled us to place in the hands of our pupils all needed books, besides purchasing a magnetic globe, and making improvements in our school-room.

I sent you a "Journal" containing our thanks to the "contributors." The next day after it was published the "Dispatch" came out in very bitter terms against northern teachers; the result of the attack upon us was to raise up warmer friends. Several of the gentlemen who contributed sent us word that they were ready to furnish more money whenever it was needed.

These children are the most impressible of any that I have ever seen. I govern them in each school, only by kind words, and better order can seldom be found among so large a number.

People say that my success has created the greatest sensation possible, we are constantly sought and persuaded to take more scholars—but feel obliged to refuse. If I had the money, I should start a Primary school in a room quite near the schoolhouse—employing a teacher from this city.

From the same.

WILMINGTON, N. C., March 22, 1867.

Everything looks hopeful and prosperous. I am not sure, but I think I shall start another school, even if the S. M. S. cannot assist me.

How? O, I feel as if it will be done! But don't want to say positively until I am sure! You know that I believe Our Father will open the way for all things which are right for me to do! I shall work, trusting in Him! I wish I could step into one of your Halls, there in Boston, and tell my simple story of the wants of the poor whites in this Southern country! I am sure I should have money enough in a very short time to establish all the schools needed in this city. Truth, facts, always move the people of New England.

From the same.

WILMINGTON, N. C., April 9, 1867.

People are beginning to visit my school, they think it wonderful with all those children that I do not have to whip any. But there is a greater power in love! "Suffer little children and forbid them not to come unto me," was the injunction of the Great Teacher, and I feel that the Spirit which He exerted, should be that which should govern my school.

From the same.

WILMINGTON, N. C., April 22, 1867.

I believe I sent you word that we received a present of $99.50 from citizens to assist in purchasing books for the school. Well, my school increased, I could not have a heart to refuse the children, until I found it necessary to have another teacher. Miss Martha Rush, of this city, took the place; and she and I have been teaching in the *same room* ever since, as I found it impossible to secure another room near the schoolhouse.

Last Tuesday I thought I would see if the gentlemen here would help me build another recitation room. The first two men whom I saw, agreed to give the lumber, another all the nails, etc. Then Mr. Kidder found a carpenter to take the job, and I must raise the sum of $125 to pay for the work. Straightway, I took a paper and five men gave $65, the rest I expect to obtain as soon as I start out again.

The whole will cost, I think, $300, lumber is dear, so you will see at once, that for the first six months it will not be well to ask for more help. Do you not think they have done well? $400 (the first four months) they have given, and that freely, because they are satisfied with the work.

People are coming in to visit us, and they express themselves freely. They seem perfectly astonished at the order we have, and that order obtained without "whipping." I wish you could see my school, the children are learning fast; one hundred and six in my day school, and one hundred and four in my Sunday school. I enjoy my work very much. The Sewing school also is well attended.

They are making a strong effort to start free schools throughout the city. One gentleman, in one of their meetings to discuss the matter, referred to Miss Bradley's school as one already fully organized, and recommended others to be started on the same plan.

It is very encouraging, and gives me great pleasure to know that my work is appreciated.

From Miss Claribel Gerrish.

WILMINGTON, N. C., March 12, 1867.

It is pitiable to see children so ignorant through neglect, not through depravity, which usually accompanies, if it is not the source of ignorance among our children at home. At least these do not seem depraved. They are sensitive to a great degree, and very impressible. Kind words govern them—the only fear that rules being that of giving up their seat to some new applicant.

The Ladies' Benevolent Society, of this city, are considering the subject of a Free School, and Sunday one of the Clergymen preached on "Education," showing the necessity of educating all classes, rich and poor together.

So the influence of our work is felt—sufficient proof to us of the feasibility of "Reconstruction through Education."

From the same.

WILMINGTON, N. C., April 19, 1867.

They look quite neat and bright, but their minds are vacant, and they are listless in recitation. It is necessary to teach them to think, to inspire them, to impart energy. After visiting nearly fifty families, we wonder that the children are so capable as they are, when their parents are so ignorant and idle, so willing to be objects of charity; when their homes are destitute of comfort, of everything in fact but the necessities of life.

Although there are so many in such a deplorable condition, we do not find that we have been preceded by any member of a Benevolent Society or any Clergyman.

III. School at Hampton.

From Miss E. D. Southwick.

Hampton, April 18, 1867.

I find that the plan of these gentlemen is: That all who are able, shall pay one dollar and a half a month; and the destitute have their tuition free. Some gentlemen will pay for several poor scholars, if possible. The school shall be made worthy of sisterhood with the Memorial System of education, and become a blessing to the ignorant, suffering mass about us.

IV. Relief of Destitution.

From Miss Ellen M. Lee.

Richmond, Va., March 29, 1867.

This noon, eight beaming faces trudged off with budgets of skirts and outside suits. The fruit of the last barrels, received a day or two since. Each of the recipients had been alarmingly ragged the last week or two, with no home means with which to renew their tatters.

In addition, a large package of stout gingham and cotton to a very intelligent Union family, who have had boys in school all winter. They could not easily put their circumstances into words, nor could I ask. But at last it came out how first, the watch Mrs. ——— had before her marriage was sold, then bedding, furniture, and all the surplus and pleasant stores and supplies which gather in comfortable circumstances. For "people now prosperous, once poor and indebted to us, would not, now the tables are turned, help us, because of my husband's well known and unfailingly expressed Unionism. So this winter he is refused work on all sides, and it *has* seemed as if we *should* starve." This I mention, that the good Sister-hoods, who make and send these supplies, may *know what* relief they are affording; that they may *realize* how it lightens some of the burdens, which, thank God, we Massachusetts women know nothing of. And when I find a refined, intelligent woman who has so borne and suffered for the stars and stripes, it is profoundly affecting, as the *needs* of life are the same, whatever the status of the individual.

From Col. James.

Gordon, Fla., March 23, 1867.

I write to let you know that the box of clothing which you sent down has been nearly all distributed. The contributors to it could have had no greater reward for the charity and kindness than the heartfelt expressions of gratitude from the people, as they received this and that article.

A poor black, whom we know to be perfectly truthful, said in a voice trembling with the feeling that he could not fully express, that the blanket that we had given him was literally the first one that he had ever received in his life. And could you know as we do the life this man of sixty years of age has led, as a slave, the incident could never be forgotten.

Your gift, coupled with one from Mrs. Forbes of Milton, so far exceeded the necessities of the whites in our immediate neighborhood, that deeming the loyalty of the blacks whom we know to be in want, as worthy of reward, we have taken the liberty of distributing much of the clothing to them. Nothing could have been better suited to their wear and tear than what you sent.

From Miss J. A. Bell.

HARKER'S ISLAND, N. C., April 25, 1867.

The members of the Soldiers' Memorial Society will please accept my sincere thanks for the valuable and timely supply of clothing. It was most assuredly a perfect *God-send*, these people were sadly destitute.

I have an army of little ragged boys and girls "working for clothes." The parents think it is "mighty hard, when things are sent to poor folks, that they cannot get them without working like niggers for them." There is no help for them, work they *must* or die. The articles are just what are needed, stout material that will not soon wear out. These children cannot earn their clothing, they think they do, which amounts to the same thing. They will prize them more highly than if they were given to them, besides it stimulates their ambition. I have a nice little lot of thirty five acres, to employ them on.

From Miss A. Aiken.

PETERSBURG, VA., May 28, 1867.

It is with great pleasure I acknowledge the receipt of your box of valuable clothing, which reached me on Friday (24th) in good order, according to invoice. We have had so very little for our school, this winter, it gives me much satisfaction to be able to do something for them before leaving. The little dresses and chemises will be so acceptable, the distribution of them will make quite a holiday of to-morrow, for both them and myself.

I was extremely glad of the larger dresses,—two of them have been given to Nelly and her daughter Peggy, who before the war were faithful house servants of a wealthy family, and were treated with unusual kindness as such, since when, being cast off, they have wandered from place to place, giving their services for the past year to some one in the country who cheated them out of their recompense. So they had still but the one *work-dress*, (or coat as they call it,) of the peculiar material formerly made for them, looking as if worn since they left "their house of bondage." Peggy's eyes sparkled with delight at the thoughts of a new dress, but Nelly's with tears, her old heart so worn with suffering and trouble that a little joy causes it to overflow.

It would be useless to repeat to you, whose hearts have opened by the knowledge of their needs and wrongs, the sad history of each recipient, but be assured that every article which your box contained will give comfort, and assist in lessening that need and suffering with which a majority of these people are still suffering, and that my heart is very grateful for the happiness of being your almoner.

Very sincerely yours,

A. AIKEN.

From Mrs. M. C. Ringgold.

CHARLESTON, S. C., Dec. 31, 1866.

The box and its contents arrived safely. They were most acceptable, particularly the dresses; two of them were given to two ladies who once were well off in the goods of this world, but who were too glad to get them.

Say to the rich ladies of Boston, that whenever they have a cast off dress, they cannot do better than send it here to the poor.

From the same.

CHARLESTON, S. C., Feb. 14, 1867.

Who are the inmates of the House of Industry?

About eighty grown people and twenty little children, many from the most respectable grades of life: one, a lady quite in advanced life, the widow of a Commodore in the navy; another, the aged widow of an old army officer; and others, who have always been plain, honest hard working people, but whose savings have become converted into confederate paper.

From the same.

CHARLESTON, S. C., June 24, 1867.

A day since, a poor freed woman came in from the country, with five children, all in a state of starvation, and *naked*, to these I gave clothing and food.

www.ingramcontent.com/pod-product-compliance
Lightning Source LLC
LaVergne TN
LVHW011133110826
845150LV00008B/2318

9781418193904